GRAPHIC HISTORY

THE STORY OF THE STATUE OF LIBERTY

by Xavier Niz

illustrated by Cynthia Martin
and Brent Schoonover

Consultant:

Barbara Truesdell, PhD

Assistant Director

Center for the Study of History and Memory

Indiana University, Bloomington, Indiana

Capstone
press

Mankato, Minnesota

Graphic Library is published by Capstone Press,
151 Good Counsel Drive, P.O. Box 669, Mankato, Minnesota 56002.
www.capstonepub.com

062011
006228WZVMI

 Books published by Capstone Press are manufactured with paper
containing at least 10 percent post-consumer waste.

Library of Congress Cataloging-in-Publication Data
Niz, Xavier.
    The story of the Statue of Liberty / by Xavier Niz; illustrated by Cynthia Martin and
Brent Schoonover.
        p. cm.—(Graphic library. Graphic history)
    Summary: "In graphic novel format, tells the story of the building of the Statue of
Liberty"—Provided by publisher.
    Includes bibliographical references and index.
    ISBN-13: 978-0-7368-5494-8 (hardcover)
    ISBN-10: 0-7368-5494-0 (hardcover)
    ISBN-13: 978-0-7368-6882-2 (softcover pbk.)
    ISBN-10: 0-7368-6882-8 (softcover pbk.)
    1. Statue of Liberty (New York, N.Y.)—Juvenile literature. 2. New York (N.Y.)—Buildings,
structures, etc.—Juvenile literature. I. Martin, Cynthia, 1961– ill. II. Schoonover, Brent, ill.
III. Title. IV. Series.
F128.64.L6N59 2006
974.7'1—dc22   2005028953

Art Direction and Design
Jason Knudson

Production Designer
Alison Thiele

Storyboard Artist
Alison Thiele

Colorist
Brent Schoonover

Editor
Christopher Harbo

Editor's note: Direct quotations from primary sources are indicated by a yellow background.

Direct quotations appear on the following pages:
Page 27, from *The Writings and Speeches of Grover Cleveland* by George F. Parker
(New York: Kraus Reprint, 1970).

TABLE of CONTENTS

Bartholdi worked on his design for the next four years.

The crown is perfect!

But the left hand needs more work.

Finally in 1875, Bartholdi showed Laboulaye his final design.

I present you with—

—Liberty Enlightening the World!

Wonderful! How tall will she stand?

150 feet!

This is a huge project. Can you handle the job?

We are ready for the challenge!

Bartholdi built several models of the statue before construction began. The largest was 36 feet tall. Workers placed a great number of small dots on this model.

It's time to take that one apart so we can start on the full-sized pieces.

The 36-foot model was split into several smaller pieces. Then, the distance between the dots on each piece was measured and multiplied by four. This gave the dimensions for the completed version of each piece.

Bartholdi went to New York after unveiling the torch. He needed to start fund-raising to pay for the statue's pedestal.

The American branch of the Franco-American Union should pay for the statue's pedestal. Will you be able to raise enough money?

The statue is popular with the people right now. Raising money shouldn't be a problem.

Have you seen the papers?!

I don't believe this!

The New York Times says that the statue will cost $2 million. And that New Yorkers will have to pay for it.

But that's not true!

15

CHAPTER 4
LIBERTY COMES HOME

While the *World* was trying to raise money, the completed statue had been on display to the public in France. Finally, in January 1885, the statue was taken apart. Each piece was numbered and packed away.

How many crates do you think it will take?

According to my list, she should fit into 214 crates.

On May 21, 1885, the statue set out for America by ship.

Load those crates carefully.

On June 17, the statue arrived in New York Harbor. The crates were unpacked and the statue was stored until the pedestal was completed.

Finally, in April 1886, reconstruction of the statue began on Bedloe's Island. Piece by piece, the statue was put together on its new home.

Later in the day, Bartholdi unveiled the face of his statue.

The day ended with a speech by President Cleveland, 21 years after the idea was first born.

We will not forget that Liberty has here made her home, nor shall her chosen altar be neglected.

In the years that followed, the statue was seen by millions of immigrants who passed through New York Harbor. For all those people, the statue stood for a chance to start a new life. The statue still stands as a symbol of freedom and independence.

MORE ABOUT THE STATUE OF LIBERTY

- Édouard de Laboulaye never lived to see his dream come true. He died on May 25, 1884, just two months before the statue was completed in France.

- The Statue of Liberty stands within the star-shaped walls of Fort Wood. Built from 1808 to 1811, Fort Wood protected part of New York Harbor for about 50 years.

- The pedestal was designed by American architect Richard Morris Hunt. Made of granite and concrete, the pedestal stands 154 feet high. When completed, its foundation was the world's largest concrete structure.

- At the time of its dedication, the Statue of Liberty was the tallest structure in New York City. Standing 305 feet (93 meters) tall, the statue remained the tallest structure until 1899 when the St. Paul's Building was built to 310 feet (94.5 meters).

- Some people believe the face of the Statue of Liberty is modeled after Frédéric-Auguste Bartholdi's mother.

The seven spikes on Liberty's crown represent the seven seas and seven continents.

 A model of the Statue of Liberty stands near the Eiffel Tower in Paris, France. This model is about one-fourth the size of the original Statue of Liberty. It was given to France in 1885 by U.S. citizens living in Paris.

Liberty's skin was made out of 300 sheets of copper. Each piece is about as thick as a penny.

The statue's nose is 4.5 feet (1.4 meters) long. Her eyes are each 2.5 feet (0.8 meter) across.

The Statue of Liberty was the color of a penny when it was built. Its copper skin turned green after many years in New York Harbor. The green color is a thin film called a patina. This film forms from a reaction between air and copper.

GLOSSARY

campaign (kam-PAYN)—a series of actions organized over a period of time in order to achieve something

pedestal (PED-es-tuhl)—the bottom support of a statue or pillar

pylon (PYE-lon)—a tall, metal tower that supports a building or structure.

resolution (rez-uh-LOO-shuhn)—a formal statement of a decision

scholar (SKOL-ur)—a person who has done advanced study in a special field

INTERNET SITES

FactHound offers a safe, fun way to find Internet sites related to this book. All of the sites on FactHound have been researched by our staff.

Here's how:

1. *Visit www.facthound.com*
2. Type in this special code **0736854940** for age-appropriate sites. Or enter a search word related to this book for a more general search.
3. Click on the **Fetch It** button.

FactHound will fetch the best sites for you!

READ MORE

Ashley, Susan. *The Statue of Liberty.* Places in American History. Milwaukee: Weekly Reader Early Learning Library, 2004.

Hochain, Serge. *Building Liberty: A Statue Is Born.* Washington, D.C.: National Geographic, 2004.

Nobleman, Marc Tyler. *The Statue of Liberty.* First Facts. American Symbols. Mankato, Minn.: Capstone Press, 2003.

Whitelaw, Nancy. *Joseph Pulitzer and the New York World.* Makers of the Media. Greensboro, N.C.: Morgan Reynolds, 2000.

BIBLIOGRAPHY

Bell, James B., and Richard I. Abrams. *In Search of Liberty: The Story of the Statue of Liberty and Ellis Island.* Garden City, N.Y.: Doubleday, 1984.

Handlin, Oscar, and the editors of the Newsweek Book Division. *Statue of Liberty.* Wonders of Man. New York: Newsweek, 1971.

Moreno, Barry. *The Statue of Liberty Encyclopedia.* New York: Simon & Schuster, 2000.

Parker, George F. *The Writings and Speeches of Grover Cleveland.* New York: Kraus Reprint, 1970.

INDEX